SEASONS

Spring

Kay Barnham

PowerKiDS
press™

New York

Published in 2011 by The Rosen Publishing Group Inc.
29 East 21st Street, New York, NY 10010

Copyright © 2011 Wayland/
The Rosen Publishing Group, Inc.

First Edition

Senior Editor: Claire Shanahan
Designer: Ruth Cowan
Picture Researcher: Louise Edgeworth
Concept Designer: Paul Cherrill

Library of Congress Cataloging-in-Publication Data

Barnham, Kay.
  Spring / Kay Barnham. — 1st ed.
      p. cm. — (Seasons)
  Includes index.
  ISBN 978-1-61532-569-6 (library binding)
  ISBN 978-1-61532-575-7 (paperback)
  ISBN 978-1-61532-852-9 (6-pack)
  1. Spring—Juvenile literature. I. Title.
  QB637.5.B37 2011
  508.2—dc22
                                    2009045760

Photographs:
Alamy: Arco Images GmbH Imprint page, David Noton Photography p4-5, Dennis Hallinan p7, Redmond Durrell p10, Nigel Cattlin p14, Arco Images GmbH p15, Foodfolio p17, Joe Fox p19; Corbis: Paul Barton p6, Yujiro Matsuo/amanaimages p8, Julia Thorne/Robert Harding World Imagery p12; Getty: American Images Inc Title page, David Seed Photography p9, Superstudio p16, American Images Inc p18; Dreamstime: © Gemphotography p11, COVER; IStockphoto: p13.

Manufactured in China
CPSIA Compliance Information: Batch #WAS0102PK: For Further Information contact Rosen Publishing, New York, New York at 1-800-237-9932

Web Sites

Due to the changing nature of Internet links, PowerKids Press has developed an online list of Web sites related to the subject of this book. This site is updated regularly. Please use this link to access this list:
http://www.powerkidslinks.com/sesn/spring

Contents

The Seasons

There are four seasons in the year.
The seasons are called spring, summer,
fall, and winter. Each season is different.

4

In the spring, the days become warmer and longer. The spring months are March, April, and May.

Spring Weather

The weather gets warmer in the spring.
The month of May can have quite a
lot of sunshine.

Early mornings can still be chilly.

At this time of year, the weather can change a lot. There may be rain, sun, wind, or snow—all on the same day!

Sudden showers are common.

Spring Trees

Spring is a time of new life. Plants, trees, and grass start to grow. Fruit trees, such as cherry trees and plum trees, grow blossoms.

The wind blows blossoms from the trees. Brand new leaves are left behind.

Seeds that fell from trees
in the fall begin to sprout.
Soon, they will grow into
tiny plants called saplings.

This is an oak sapling. Oak trees may live up to a thousand years!

Spring Flowers

In the spring, lots of flowers appear. First, shoots push up through the soil. Then the stems grow tall.

Buds open to show the beautiful petals inside.

petals

bud

stem

English bluebells flower in the late spring in some parts of the country. They grow in woods and forests.

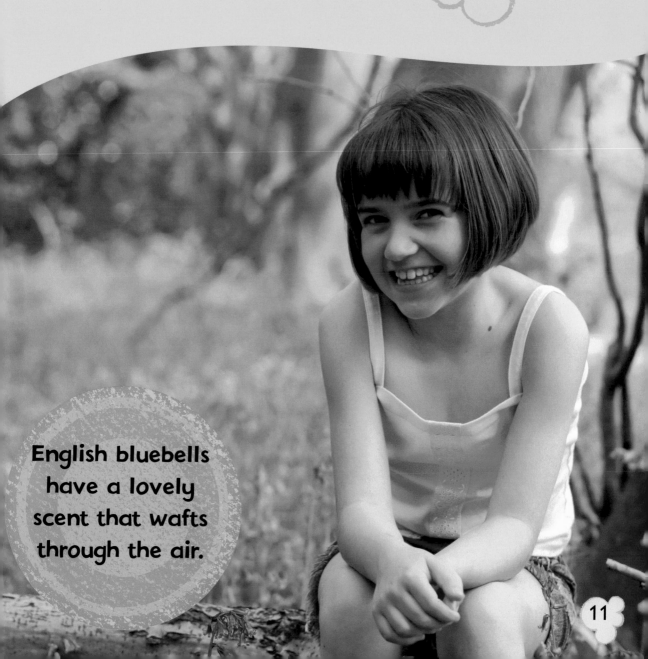

English bluebells have a lovely scent that wafts through the air.

Spring Animals

Spring is the time of year when lambs are born. A lamb drinks milk from its mother. When it is older, it will eat grass.

A ewe is pregnant for about five months before giving birth to lambs.

Baby birds hatch from eggs.
The mother brings her chicks food
to eat. When the chicks grows bigger,
they will find their own food.

Birds' nests can be made of twigs, grass, and leaves.

Fun in the Spring

Spring is an exciting time to explore
the countryside. Look for frogspawn
in ponds or streams. Frogspawn is a mass
of frog's eggs.

Each black dot takes three or four months to turn into a fro

Spring is a good time to visit a farm. There, you will see many baby animals, such as piglets, calves, ducklings, and chicks.

How many ducklings can you see?

15

Spring Food

Spring is the best time to plant vegetables such as carrots, peas, and potatoes.

Seeds and seedlings must be watered often, so they grow.

At this time of year, rhubarb is ripe and ready to eat.

Rhubarb can be made into delicious desserts such as this rhubarb pie.

17

Spring Festivals

In the United States and Canada, spring happens near the beginning of the year. The festivals of Easter and Passover are both celebrated in the spring.

Have you ever taken part in an Easter-egg hunt?

On March 17, Irish people around the world celebrate St. Patrick's Day. St. Patrick is the patron saint of Ireland.

These people are taking part in a St. Patrick's Day parade.

Why Do We Have Seasons?

We have seasons because Earth is tilted. As Earth moves around the Sun, different parts of the planet are nearer the Sun.

In the **spring**, our part of the planet moves toward the Sun. The weather grows warmer.

In the **summer**, our part of the planet is nearest the Sun, so the weather is hot.

In the **fall**, our part of the planet moves away from the Sun. The weather grows cooler.

In the **winter**, our part of the planet is farthest from the Sun. This means that the weather is cold.

It takes a year for the four seasons
to happen. This is because it takes
a year for Earth to move around the Sun.

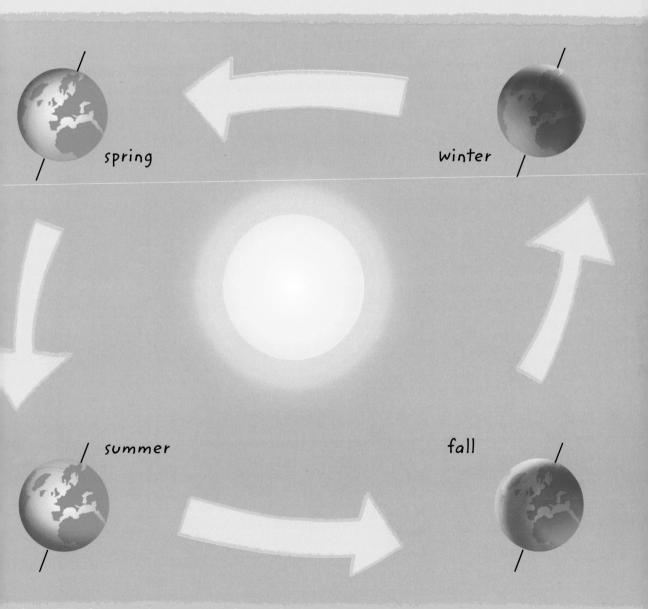

spring

winter

summer

fall

Make a Weather Chart

You will ne
- a piece of c
- a ruler
- colored pen
- a clock or wo
- a measuring
- a thermome

Keep a record of the weather in the spring.

1. Draw a calendar for each month of spring, with a box for each day.

2. On each day, record whether it has been sunny, cloudy, rainy, or snowy. Use a symbol for each kind of weather.

3. If it has been sunny, write down how many hours of sun there were.

22

4. Leave a measuring cup outside. If it has been raining, check the measuring cup to see how many inches of rain have fallen.

5. Each day, check your thermometer and write down how warm or cold it has been.

6. At the end of each month, look back at your chart. You might be surprised at how many different types of weather there have been!

Glossary and Further Information

blossoms the flowers on a tree
ewe a female sheep
patron a saint who is thought of as protecting a place or activity
petal one of the colored parts of a flower
pregnant when an animal or human is expecting a baby
sapling a young tree
seedling a young plant, often grown from a seed
shoot a new part of a plant
sprout to begin to grow
stem the main part of a plant, which grows above the ground

Books

Spring
by Nuria Roca
(Barrons Educational, 2004)
Spring
by Sian Smith
(Heinemann Library, 2009)
Watching the Seasons
by Edana Eckart
(Children's Press, 2004)

Index